12/16

SWIMMING
WITH
SHARKS

The Daring Discoveries of
Eugenie Clark

Heather Lang

pictures by
Jordi Solano

Albert Whitman & Company
Chicago, Illinois

Little Genie stood on the railing and pressed her face against the mysterious glass tank.

Most people saw piercing eyes…rows of sharp teeth…vicious, bloodthirsty killers!

Not Eugenie Clark. She saw sleek, graceful fish gliding through the water. She longed to be inside the tank…on the bottom of the ocean…swimming with sharks.

Every Saturday morning, Genie raced into the New York Aquarium and shared her passion with anyone who would listen.

Genie loved learning about all kinds of fish, but there wasn't much information about sharks. She dreamed someday she'd discover their secrets too.

Mama saved her pennies and bought Genie her own fish tank.

Soon their small apartment overflowed with fish and reptiles.

Genie wondered, *Do fish get sick? Do they think? Do they sleep?*

She observed. She sketched. She took detailed notes.

Genie dreamed of becoming a fish scientist and exploring the ocean like her hero William Beebe.

"Maybe you should take up typing and you could be a secretary to William Beebe," Mama suggested. In the 1930s, few people dared to study the depths of the sea, and none were women. Most people didn't think women could be scientists or explorers.

"I don't want to be anybody's secretary!" Genie said.

Gene took every science class she could find in college and got her master's degree in zoology. When a famous ichthyologist—a fish scientist—asked her to come to California to be his research assistant and take oceanography classes, she jumped at the chance.

Sharks are complex

first dorsal fin →

second dorsal fin

nostril

gill openings

← pectoral fin

pelvic fin

caudal fin

The ocean became her classroom! Genie collected fish and studied them. She took water samples. She dissected a swell shark to investigate how and why it puffs up.

Wearing a face mask, Genie explored the underwater world for the first time. Its beauty mesmerized her. Genie couldn't wait to dive deeper, stay under water longer, and maybe even see some sharks.

One day, on a research trip, Genie's professor let her try helmet
diving. As she slipped into the cold water, the heavy metal helmet
pressed on her shoulders. A line from the helmet attached to an air
pump in the boat.

Down…down…The kelp welcomed her, waving back and forth with the underwater currents.

Down…down…down…

She marveled at the fish all around her. Genie was finally on the bottom of the ocean!

In 1949 the US Navy hired Genie to study poisonous fish in the South Seas. One afternoon while collecting fish underwater she sensed something behind her.

A huge shark!

Genie froze.

The shark swam closer…and closer…a few feet away…
Then suddenly it turned and dove down, disappearing into the darkness.
Genie was too excited to be scared.
Most people thought sharks were stupid, unpredictable eating machines.
Genie believed there must be more to these beautiful fish.

Most sharks are timid

In 1955 she opened the Cape Haze Marine Laboratory in Florida. Right away she built a shark pen next to the dock. No one had studied living sharks in their natural environment before.

Genie caught hammerheads, blacktip sharks, dogfish sharks, lemon sharks, nurse sharks, bull sharks, and tiger sharks.

Sharks are diverse

She observed. She sketched. She took detailed notes.
The more time Genie spent with sharks, the more she knew people were wrong about them. She wondered, *Could sharks be trained?*

In no time Genie taught a pair of lemon sharks to press a white board connected to an underwater bell, then swim to another spot to catch their reward. The female shark discovered if she let the male press the target, she could gobble up the food before he got there.

Even after a ten-week break, the sharks remembered the drill right away.

Sharks are clever

Scientists all over the world admired Genie's research and came to work with the "Shark Lady" at her lab.

As diving equipment improved, Genie dove deeper. She spent longer periods of time underwater and uncovered more secrets about sharks.

Genie studied the mating frenzy of the grey reef shark.

She researched an undersea hatchery for the Japanese swell shark.

She swam with a dogfish shark, as small as a pencil, and a whale shark, as big as a bus.

Some sharks
are gentle

Genie knew the more she discovered about sharks, the less people would fear them.

When she heard there might be "sleeping sharks" in Mexico, she had to investigate. Scientists thought sharks had to be swimming to keep oxygen flowing through their mouths and over their gills. She wondered, *Why would a shark lie still?*

Down, down, down, she swam into the sharks' cave. Suddenly she was face-to-face with a requiem shark, one of the world's most feared fish.

Was the shark really sleeping? Would it feel trapped in the cave and attack?

Genie stared at the shark's sharp biting teeth and the four rows of extra teeth behind them. The shark's mouth opened and closed, opened and closed, pumping oxygen over its gills. A remora fish cleaned the shark, nibbling on parasites and wiggling in and out of its gills.

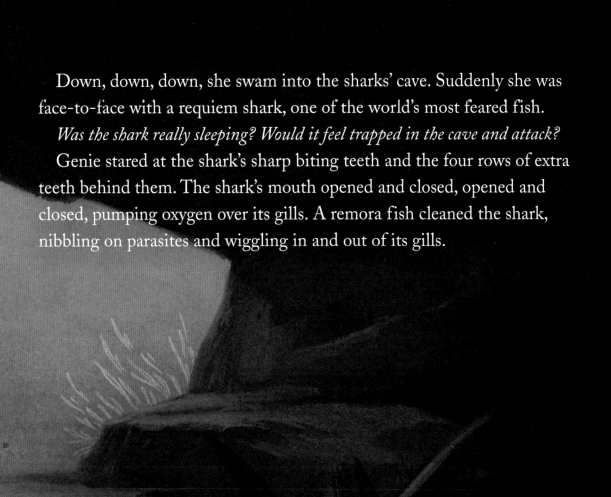

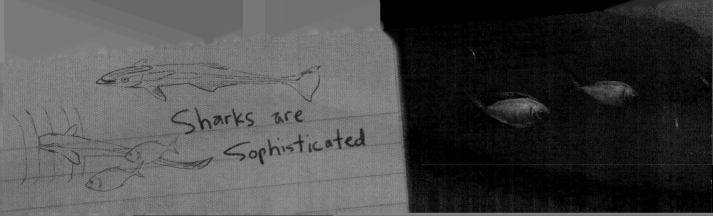

Sharks are
Sophisticated

As Genie swam toward the shark, it followed her with its eyes. This shark was not sleeping!

But it did not attack.

She took water samples and tested rocks and water currents.

She observed. She sketched. She took detailed notes.

Genie discovered the water in the caves was less salty, loosening parasites on the shark and making cleaning easier for the remoras. These underwater caves were cleaning stations for sharks!

The more time Genie spent underwater, the fewer sharks she saw. People killed them out of fear. People killed them for their fins. People killed them thinking it would make beaches safer. Sharks had ruled the oceans for more than 400 million years, and now they were in serious danger.

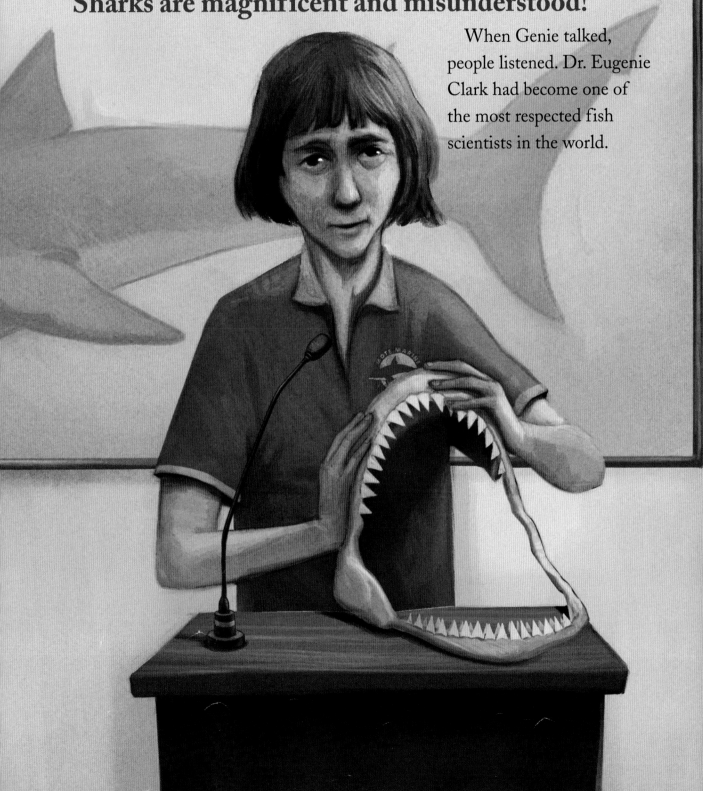

Genie's research proved that sharks were not voracious killers. She knew most sharks should be more afraid of us than we are of them.

Genie spoke out to the world:

"Sharks are magnificent and misunderstood!"

When Genie talked, people listened. Dr. Eugenie Clark had become one of the most respected fish scientists in the world.

And after her decades of research and discoveries, Genie knew, "there are lots of things—big things—that we don't know about. There will always be more to learn. Always more surprises."

She never stopped pressing her face against the glass and wondering...

Author's Note

As a young girl I saw the shark movie *Jaws*, and a fear of sharks followed me into adulthood. My fear drew me to this story of an open-minded woman who didn't judge sharks based on rumors or appearance. She not only dared to swim with sharks but followed a career path that few people—men or women—had the courage to pursue.

Genie experienced discrimination both as a woman and a Japanese American. Columbia turned her down for graduate school because she was a woman. Instead she got a job in a chemistry lab and took night classes at New York University. Later Genie was denied the opportunity to attend overnight research trips because she was a woman. Once, the government hired her to do research in the Philippines but wouldn't clear her passport because of her Japanese heritage. Genie never let the discrimination bring her down—she always kept moving forward. She believed these experiences helped make her "aggressive and spunky," traits that served her well in her career.

I was struck deeply by Genie's intense wonder about the ocean and its inhabitants. Her curiosity drove her to study all kinds of fish. She researched filefish that changed color, puffer fish, mysterious garden eels, and poisonous fish. She published over 175 articles about fish and made seventy-two submersible dives. For twenty-three years she taught at the University of Maryland and won countless honors and medals—all while raising four children!

When Genie passed away in 2015 at the age of ninety-two, the world lost an exceptional scientist and an even better person. I am so grateful I had the chance to meet with her at the Mote Marine Laboratory and Aquarium in Sarasota, Florida. Having read about the little Cape Haze Marine Laboratory she founded in 1955, I was overwhelmed by the scope and size of this now world-renowned research center and aquarium. Genie's office, filled with books, pictures, shark jaws, and other mementos, revealed the depth of her past adventures. At age ninety-one, after eighty years of researching fish, her eyes sparkled as she described her upcoming research trip to the Solomon Islands, where she would study the spotted oceanic triggerfish and get in a dive or two!

More about Sharks

Long before dinosaurs roamed the earth, sharks populated the oceans. They remained unthreatened at the top of the food chain until humans invaded their home. We pollute oceans with trash, oil, and nylon fishing lines. We overfish and use destructive fishing methods. We wrongly believe sharks are a significant threat to humans and kill them unnecessarily. In China and other parts of Asia, many people think shark fins make good soup and have special healing powers, so millions of sharks are killed every year to support the shark fin trade. Some of the almost 400 species of sharks are now on the verge of extinction.

Changing the shark's reputation as a cold, voracious killer is a challenging task. As Dr. Clark pointed out, just because they can't change the expression on their faces doesn't mean they aren't thinking or feeling. "Very few people are ever attacked by sharks," said Dr. Clark. Sharks attack humans if they feel threatened or when they mistake humans for prey. Most shark attacks are bite and release as sharks have no interest in eating humans.

Sharks also play a surprising role in keeping the planet healthy. They are part of the delicate food chain that allows for the existence of phytoplankton, a plant in the ocean that creates our oxygen. More than half of the air we breathe comes from the oceans.

Sharks are an irreplaceable part of the earth's ecosystem. Thanks to the work of Dr. Clark and other fish scientists, people are beginning to realize that sharks deserve our respect and protection.

Photos from left to right: Dr. Clark examines a shark caught on a fisherman's baited hook in Mexico, 1974; on the Cape Haze Marine Laboratory dock, Dr. Clark records measurements of a bull shark; Dr. Clark studies fish in the Gulf of Aqaba (circa 1950)

Acknowledgments

I am so grateful to the late Eugenie Clark and her assistant, Rachel Dreyer, for answering my many questions, sending photos and articles, meeting with me, and reviewing the manuscript. A special thank-you to Genie's son, Tak Konstantinou, and Dr. Robert Hueter, Director for the Center for Shark Research at Mote Marine Laboratory, for their research assistance, and to my editor, Wendy McClure, for her outstanding advice and feedback.

Selected Sources

Butts, Ellen, and Schwartz, Joyce R. *Eugenie Clark: Adventures of a Shark Scientist*. North Haven, CT: Linnet Books, 2000.

Clark, Eugenie, "Into the Lairs of 'Sleeping' Sharks," *National Geographic*, April 1975, 571–584.

_____. *The Lady and the Sharks*. Sarasota, FL: Peppertree Press, 2010.

_____. *Lady with a Spear*. New York: Harper & Brothers, 1953.

_____. "Sharks: Magnificent and Misunderstood," *National Geographic*, August 1981, 138–187.

McGovern, Ann. *Adventures of the Shark Lady: Eugenie Clark Around the World*. New York: Scholastic, 1998.

_____. *Shark Lady: The True Adventures of Eugenie Clark*. New York: Four Winds Press, 1978.

McGovern, Ann, and Clark, Eugenie. *The Desert Beneath the Sea*. New York: Scholastic, 1991.

Ross, Michael Elsohn. *Fish Watching with Eugenie Clark*. Minneapolis: Carolrhoda Books, 2000.

For Jenny—HL

To my dad—JS

Library of Congress Cataloging-in-Publication
data is on file with the publisher.

Text copyright © 2016 by Heather Lang
Pictures copyright © 2016 by Albert Whitman & Company
Pictures by Jordi Solano
Photos courtesy of Mote Marine Laboratory
Published in 2016 by Albert Whitman & Company
ISBN 978-0-8075-2187-8

Printed in China
10 9 8 7 6 5 4 3 2 1 LP 24 23 22 21 20 19 18 17 16

Design by Jordan Kost

For more information about Albert Whitman & Company,
visit our web site at www.albertwhitman.com.